What Happens in Spring:

Gardens in Spring

by Jenny Fretland VanVoorst

Bullfrog
Books

Ideas for Parents and Teachers

Bullfrog Books let children practice reading informational text at the earliest reading levels. Repetition, familiar words, and photo labels support early readers.

Before Reading

- Discuss the cover photo. What does it tell them?
- Look at the picture glossary together. Read and discuss the words.

Read the Book

- "Walk" through the book and look at the photos. Let the child ask questions. Point out the photo labels.
- Read the book to the child, or have him or her read independently.

After Reading

- Prompt the child to think more. Ask: Have you ever planted a garden? What did you grow?

Bullfrog Books are published by Jump!
5357 Penn Avenue South
Minneapolis, MN 55419
www.jumplibrary.com

Library of Congress Cataloging-in-Publication Data

Fretland VanVoorst, Jenny, 1972– author.
 Gardens in spring / by Jenny Fretland VanVoorst.
  pages cm. — (What happens in spring?)
 "Bullfrog Books are published by Jump!."
 Summary: "This photo-illustrated book for beginning readers discusses the experience of gardening in springtime, from preparing the soil and planting seeds to nurturing new growth. Includes picture glossary and index."
—Provided by publisher.
 Audience: Ages 5–8
 Audience: K to grade 3
 ISBN 978-1-62031-236-0 (hardcover: alk. paper)
 ISBN 978-1-62031-480-7 (paperback)
 ISBN 978-1-62496-323-0 (ebook)
1. Gardens—Juvenile literature.
2. Gardening—Juvenile literature.
3. Spring—Juvenile literature. I. Title.
 SB457.F68 2016
 635—dc23
                                    2014048517

Series Designer: Ellen Huber
Book Designer: Michelle Sonnek
Photo Researcher: Michelle Sonnek

Photo Credits: All photos by Shutterstock except: age fotostock, 4, 8–9, 16–17, 22bl, 23br; Getty, 17, 22br; iStock, 3; SuperStock, 5; Thinkstock, 10, 22tl.

Printed in the United States of America at Corporate Graphics in North Mankato, Minnesota.

Table of Contents

Spring Gardens

Spring is here!

It's time to
start a garden.
What should
we grow?

Let's plant peas!

spade

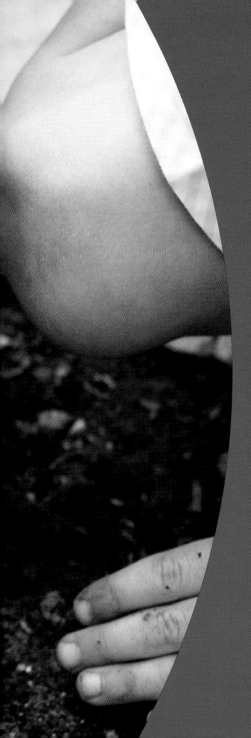

Ann takes a spade.

She loosens the soil.

Tad makes a hole.
Plop! He drops in
a seed.

seeds

Lia finds a watering can.

She sprinkles water
on the soil.

Now they must wait.

The sun shines down.

It warms the soil.

Under the ground
the seed sprouts.

It becomes a plant.

Pat pulls up weeds.
Eva waters the soil.

17

The plants get bigger.

Look! Pea pods are growing on the vine.

It's time to pick them.
Yum! Let's eat.

In the Garden

seeds

pea pods

spade

watering can

Picture Glossary

soil
Dirt or earth in which plants grow.

sprout
When a plant sprouts, it starts to grow and produce shoots or buds.

sprinkle
To scatter something in small drops or bits.

weeds
Plants that are seen as useless or harmful and grow where they are not wanted.

Index

To Learn More

Learning more is as easy as 1, 2, 3.

1) Go to www.factsurfer.com

2) Enter "gardensinspring" into the search box.

3) Click the "Surf" button to see a list of websites.

With factsurfer.com, finding more information is just a click away.